King of Hell Vol. 11
Written by Ra In-Soo
Illustrated by Kim Jae-Hwan

Translation - Lauren Na
English Adaptation - R.A. Jones
Copy Editors - Suzanne Waldman and Peter Ahlstrom
Retouch and Lettering - James Lee
Production Artist - Gloria Wu
Graphic Design - James Lee
Cover Design - Seth Cable

Editor - Rob Tokar
Digital Imaging Manager - Chris Buford
Production Managers - Jennifer Miller and Mutsumi Miyazaki
Managing Editor - Lindsey Johnston
VP of Production - Ron Klamert
Publisher and E.I.C. - Mike Kiley
President and C.O.O. - John Parker
C.E.O. - Stuart Levy

A 🔴 TOKYOPOP® Manga

TOKYOPOP Inc.
5900 Wilshire Blvd. Suite 2000
Los Angeles, CA 90036

E-mail: info@TOKYOPOP.com
Come visit us online at www.TOKYOPOP.com

ISBN: 1-59816-059-1

First TOKYOPOP printing: November 2005
10 9 8 7 6 5 4 3 2 1
Printed in the USA

VOLUME II

BY
RA IN-SOO
&
KIM JAE-HWAN

HAMBURG // LONDON // LOS ANGELES // TOKYO

MAJEH:

When he was alive, Majeh was an extremely powerful and much-feared warrior. In death, Majeh was recruited to be a collector of souls for the King of Hell. Recently, Majeh was returned to his human form in order to destroy escaped evil spirits for the King of Hell. There are two catches, however: Majeh's full powers are restrained by a mystical seal and his physical form is that of a teenage boy.

CHUNG POONG NAMGOONG:

A coward from a once-respected family, Chung Poong left home hoping to prove himself at the Martial Arts Tournament in Nakyang. Broke and desperate, Chung Poong tried to rob Majeh. In a very rare moment of pity, Majeh allowed Chung Poong to live...and to tag along with him to the tournament.

DOHWA BAIK:

A vivacious vixen whose weapons of choice are poisoned needles. After repeatedly humiliating the hapless trio known as the Insane Hounds, she joined Majeh and Chung Poong on the way to the tournament.

KING OF HELL:

You were expecting horns and a pitchfork? This benevolent, otherworldly ruler reigns over the souls of the dead like a shepherd tending his flock.

SAMHUK:

Originally sent by the King of Hell to spy on the unpredictable Majeh, Samhuk was quickly discovered and now--much to his dismay--acts as the warrior's ghostly manservant.

THE MARTIAL ARTS CHILD PRODIGIES

DOHAK:
A 15-year-old monk and a master at fighting with a rod, he was affiliated with the Sorim Temple in the Soong mountains. After being kidnapped, Dohak was transformed into a fighting zombie of the Soo Ra Hyur Chun sect, making him a blood-craving killing machine who retained the fighting abilities he'd developed when he was alive. When Dohak was ordered to attack Majeh, Majeh had no choice but to slay the young monk. True to form, Dohak thanked Majeh with his dying breath.

YOUNG:
A 15-year-old sword-master possessing incredible speed, he is affiliated with Mooyoung Moon--a clan of assassins 500 strong. After seeing Majeh defeat the demon-possessed master at the martial arts tournament, Young admitted he has no interest in fighting Majeh...though Young's curiosity has driven the youthful assassin to accompany Majeh on his current mission.

POONG CHUN:
A 12-year-old expert with the broadsword, he is affiliated with the Shaman Sect. Poong Chun is the "uncle" (martial arts superior) of Chun Hae--Chung Poong's older brother. As a direct result of Chun Hae's abuse of Chung Poong, Majeh took great pains to publicly torture and humiliate Poong Chun at the tournament. Poong Chun was apparently kidnapped along with most of the other young martial arts prodigies.

CRAZY DOG:
A 6-year-old club-wielding hellion from a remote village, Crazy Dog lived up to his name right up to the moment of his death at the hands of a demon-possessed martial arts master.

BABY:
A 15-year-old from the infamous Blood Sect, Baby is several warriors in one...thanks to his multiple personality disorder. Baby is shy, gentle, and blushing; Hyur-ah is intense, unforgiving, and murderous; and Kwang is even scarier than Hyur-ah. The question remains: who--or what--else is also inside this young man?

CHUNG HAE:
Chung Poong's older brother and Poong Chun's martial arts "nephew" (inferior). Recently, Chung Hae went out of his way to publicly shame Chung Poong, and Majeh's subsequent humiliation of Poong Chun certainly didn't improve the brothers' relationship. Chung Hae was apparently kidnapped along with most of the other young martial arts prodigies.

MO YOUNG BAIK:

Self-described master of all the martial arts and host of the Nakyang Martial Arts Tournament. Though Mo Young has only a small understanding of Majeh's abilities, he has still placed his trust in Hell's cockiest envoy.

MR SECRETARY:

Mo-Young's subordinate, who seems to have a lot more brewing than any good secretary should.

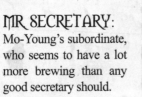

HUNTER:

A demon hunter of the Chung Myun Hhk Soo, little is known about Hunter (as he's known thus far) except that he's in his twenties, he's a little sensitive about his age, and he's an incredible fighter who's so afraid of bugs that they make him scream like a little girl.

What the Hell...?

Hell's worst inmates have escaped and fled to Earth. Seeking recently-deceased bodies to host their bitter souls, these malevolent master fighters are part of an evil scheme that could have dire consequences for both This World and the Next World. It is believed that the escaped fiends are hunting for bodies of martial arts experts, as only bodies trained in martial arts would be capable of properly employing their incredible skills.

To make matters even more difficult, the otherworldly energy emitted by the fugitives will dissipate within one month's time...after which, they will be indistinguishable from normal humans and undetectable to those from the Next World. The King of Hell has assigned Majeh to hunt down Hell's Most Wanted and return them to the Next World...but Majeh doesn't always do exactly what he's told.

Majeh was a master swordsman in life and, in death, he serves as an envoy for the King of Hell, escorting souls of the dead to the Next World. Majeh caught Samhuk--a servant for the King of Hell--spying on him and, after making the appropriate threats, now uses Samhuk as his own servant as well.

The King of Hell has reunited Majeh's spirit with his physical body, which was perfectly preserved for 300 years. Due to the influence of a Superhuman Strength Sealing Symbol (designed to keep the rebellious and powerful Majeh in check), Majeh's physical form has reverted to a teenaged state. Even with the seal in place, however, Majeh is still an extremely formidable warrior.

Along with the young, wannabe-warrior called Chung Poong Namgoong and a beautiful femme fatale named Dohwa Baik, Majeh has made his way to the much-heralded Martial Arts Tournament at Nakyang--the most likely place for the warrior demons to make their appearance.

Shortly after arriving in Nakyang, Majeh and company met Chung Hae--Chung Poong's older brother--though it was far from a happy reunion. Chung Hae berated his younger sibling and ordered Chung Poong to return home. With Majeh backing him up, Chung Poong was able to stand his ground and stay for the tournament.

Though Majeh seemed to have forgotten his mission to capture Hell's Most Wanted, the escaped evil souls certainly had not forgotten him! While Majeh faced off against Crazy Dog, the tournament was suddenly interrupted. An elderly, one-armed martial arts master--whose body was inhabited by one of the fugitive demons--forced his way into the arena and effortlessly killed Crazy Dog and Abaek. Despite his best efforts, Majeh also seemed on the verge of total defeat...though, as his life-force dissipated, the Superhuman Strength Scaling spell that limits his abilities was broken!

Freed from restraint, Majeh rose and easily obliterated his opponent. Though Majeh recovered very quickly from his battle injuries, he was still surprised to learn that, while he was out, his fellow contestants--including Chung Poong's older brother-- were kidnapped. Chung Poong and Dohwa practically begged to accompany Majeh on his search for the missing martial arts prodigies, but Majeh was only prepared to allow them to do so if they performed a mission for him first.

Realizing that Dohwa and Chung Poong were too vulnerable when facing opponents like the one-armed master, Majeh sent the pair to a cave containing a secret magic tablet. The tablet can greatly enhance the martial arts abilities and inner energy of anyone...provided they can survive its brain-twisting illusions and soul-wrenching phantoms.

Reasoning that Chung Poong and Dohwa courted death if they remained with him at their current power levels, Majeh decided it was worth risking their lives to increase their abilities. However, in typical fashion, Majeh neglected to tell the duo about the risks before they left.

Meanwhile, Majeh and the Mooyoung Moon assassin known as Young searched for the missing martial arts prodigies and discovered a diabolical plot to transform the kidnapped martial arts prodigies into zombies and start a war between the Black and White sects. The architects of this evil plan appear to be the Sa Gok, a vicious, powerful group that almost brought down the entire martial arts world fifty years ago. Unfortunately, most of the sects believe the Sa Gok were utterly eradicated... which means they can only blame each other for their missing children.

After reporting their findings to Mo Young, Majeh and Young ventured to Devil Mountain to explore a tomb that had the town talking about treasure. At the entrance to the tomb, they found many warriors fighting to keep each other out. Eventually, many different groups entered and Majeh and Young followed the powerful fighter known as Hunter into the depths of the tomb. After fighting their way through many elaborate traps, all of the fighters found themselves in a central chamber, surrounded by animated corpses that kept rising no matter how severely they were wounded. Majeh and co. feigned defeat in order to draw out the people behind the animated corpses.

After a violent confrontation, Majeh and his companions made it out of the mountain, only to discover that the White and Black Sects were lining up for battle on a nearby plain. Without a moment's hesitation, Majeh decided to fight them all--one at a time. As quickly as fighters from each Sect would step up to face him, Hell's cockiest envoy would smack them down. And he's still going...

...IN THE BLINK OF AN EYE HAVE BECOME MERE **SPECTATORS**, GAWKING AT SOME SORT OF MEDICINE MAN.

NEXT!

WITH HIS INCREDIBLE MARTIAL ARTS SKILLS, MAJEH HAS ALTERED THE COURSE OF THE DAY!

THAT BOY!

*Serpent

THANK YOU, MAJEH!

105

POOR
CHUNG
POONG.

MERCIFUL HEART OF BUDDHA!

THIS IS GETTING US NOWHERE!

DAMMIT!

IF I HAVE TO USE MY *HEAVEN'S ARROWS OF JUDGMENT* ON ALL OF THESE ZOMBIES, MY BODY WON'T BE ABLE TO WITHSTAND THE STRAIN!

YOU SPEAK OF MY BROTHER. WAS IT YOU WHO KILLED HIM?!

IF SO-- YOU'LL PAY DEARLY!

AHH. YOU WERE TWINS.

YOU ARE MY MORTAL ENEMY! THERE'S NOT ROOM FOR BOTH YOU AND I TO LIVE UNDER THE SAME SKY...!

YO. SETTLE DOWN, BIG BOY.

SURE, I HIT YOUR BROTHER A COUPLE OF TIMES--BUT IN THE END, HE COMMITTED SUICIDE!

YOU LIE!!

DAMMIT! IT'S YOU BASTARDS WHO HAVE CRIMES TO ANSWER FOR HERE!

......

......

HEH HEH...

MAYBE WE WERE TOO EASY ON HIM...

TO BE CONTINVED

IN THE NEXT VOLUME OF

KING of HELL

All out war between
the Sects and their
loved ones! Will the
Insane Hounds live
up to their names by
staying and fighting or
will they show a little sense
and run away with their tails
between their legs? And
what's Majeh's role in all of
this?

Find out in volume 12!

TOKYOPOP SHOP

WWW.TOKYOPOP.COM/SHOP

HOT NEWS!
Check out the TOKYOPOP SHOP!
The world's best collection of manga in English is now available online in one place!

DRAMACON and other hot titles are available at the store that never closes!

SAMURAI CHAMPLOO

KINGDOM HEARTS

DRAMACON

- **LOOK FOR SPECIAL OFFERS**
- **PRE-ORDER UPCOMING RELEASES**
- **COMPLETE YOUR COLLECTIONS**

A MIDNIGHT™ OPERA

Immortality, Redemption, and Bittersweet Love...

For nearly a millennium, undead creatures have blended into a Europe driven by religious dogma...

Ein DeLaLune is an underground Goth metal sensation on the Paris music scene, tragic and beautiful. He has the edge on other Goth music powerhouses—he's undead, a fact he's kept hidden for centuries. But his newfound fame might just bring out the very phantoms of his past from whom he has been hiding for centuries, including his powerful brother, Leroux. And if the two don't reconcile, the entire undead nation could rise up from the depths of modern society to lay waste to mankind.

MARK OF THE SUCCUBUS

BY ASHLY RAITI & IRENE FLORES

Maeve, a succubus-in-training, is sent to the human world to learn how to hone her skills of seduction. But things get complicated when she sets her sights on Aiden, a smart but unmotivated student at her new high school. Meanwhile, the Demon World has sent a spy to make sure Maeve doesn't step out of line. And between Aiden's witchy girlfriend, his nutty best friend, and Demon World conspiracies, Maeve is going to be lucky to make it out of our world alive!

Here is a Gothic romantic fantasy set in one of the most menacing worlds known to humans: high school.

T
TEEN
AGE 13+

BY FUYUMI SORYO

MARS

I used to do the English adaptation for *MARS* and loved working on it. The art is just amazing—Fuyumi Soryo draws these stunning characters and beautiful backgrounds to boot. I remember this one spread in particular where Rei takes Kira on a ride on his motorcycle past this factory, and it's all lit up like Christmas and the most gorgeous thing you've ever seen—and it's a factory! And the story is a super-juicy soap opera that kept me on the edge of my seat just dying to get the next volume every time I'd finish one.

~Elizabeth Hurchalla, Sr. Editor

BY SHOHEI MANABE

DEAD END

Everyone I've met who has read *Dead End* admits to becoming immediately immersed and obsessed with Shohei Manabe's unforgettable manga. If David Lynch, Clive Barker and David Cronenberg had a love child that was forced to create a manga in the bowels of a torture chamber, then *Dead End* would be the fruit of its labor. The unpredictable story follows a grungy young man as he pieces together shattered fragments of his past. Think you know where it's going? Well, think again!

~Troy Lewter, Editor